Table of Contents

# INTRODUCTION

Walter Anderson once said "our lives improve only when we step ahead to take chances- and the first and most thriving risk we can take is to be honest with ourselves" I'd like to start by congratulating you- for purchasing the Magnetic Personality- a guide that has been designed based on various researches conducted on how you can become instantly likeable and captivating. I've gone through hours of research and writing to make your life better, so now you have to step slightly outside your comfort zone, and be honest with yourself- this way, you will stand a chance of being a better person after reading this. So, what I'm trying to say is that if you're serious about being successful at everything you do in life, if you're serious about turning out to be a person who exudes personal charm and charisma, than you have to take ACTIONS with what you'll learn in this book. Let's go through this together- I want you to believe that everything you've gone through up till now; any lack of respect that might have been shown by people, any lack of ability at forming friendships, any difficulty getting your opinion across to others- none of this has been your fault, just believe that you did the best that you could do with you know. Not only that, that this is the journey you were meant to be on. Give in to it, embrace it, and love yourself as you are right here, right now. You need to understand this because in order for other people to love you, you have to love yourself as you are right now. Have you even thought about it? - That likeability is not a genetic trait? I used to think that way, like I was born with low social skills. But the fact that I've been able to totally not only improve my social abilities but become the kind of human who people gravitate to, has proven to me that this whole magnetic personality can be learned and it's my duty to let you know about it. Get it- no one is born as the next head or state or president of the United States or as a future movie star or CEO from birth. People learn how to translate what other people want to hear and see, and then deliver it with precision, how to make a killer first impression and then keep it on the move day after day- that's how it works, you can do the same thing- all you need to do is sit back and relax, take a good look at what people like in other people and compare with that factor that is holding you back.

# CHAPTER ONE

## WE ALL WANT TO BE LIKED? SHOULDN'T THERE BE A REASON FOR THAT?

Have you ever wondered, why? The response you get when you ask anyone on the street whether they want to be liked is always an emphatic yes. The truth is that very few of us can think of a better reason why we want to be liked, although in reality, there are numerous reasons- socially, professionally, and romantically- that drive us as humans to seek the interest of our fellow ones. I guess it's probably because we want to feel validated, admired and special. We want to establish a connection with other people who understand what we are going through, we feel we're social and so we need a network of others to spend time with, or probably because we want to experience the best of life as much as possible and become energized by others to make ourselves better; or simply put, we like to be liked. Being likable is far from getting something out of other people, even though it can have a big impact on how likely a friend or relative is to help you out.

Likeability also actually results in attitudes that reduces the likelihood of heart disease, stress related illnesses and overall displeasure. What you're about to learn will not only assist you to make new friends and perform better at work, but will also help you feel better. Literally, you'd be able to step up on your body's ability to combat various diseases and stay balanced on a daily basis. Is that not just fine? And science alone has not made likeability a powerful goal to attain. For a very long time now, likeability has been the main key to success in almost every area of life. It has been the only factor that every winning candidate has taken an edge in. you plan to be president? Better be more likeable than your opponent. Everyone wants likeable to be in charge, that's why they always win. Even without the knowledge of a single thing about them, likeable people attract the mind and soul of every one because they take on the role of the perpetual David to whichever Goliath happens to come forward as their opponent. Still on that, a lot of us feel meek and underappreciated, or generally trod upon by bigger and stronger people. This means that likeability is just an extension of our own self- image. We should only like that which we aspire to be and which we can easily relate to. Same with every other person, then you can become the ideal friend, partner, family member or co- worker and also the most likeable human in the room.

Likeability is just like joining the team- a person everyone loves and admires who has something amazingly valuable to offer. It could be your sense of humor, or your ability to talk to relate with anyone about anything. In order to really begin using the techniques and exercises you'll find in this guide, I have found this one exercise in particular to be a powerful beginner exercise to start practicing. It will make you shift your perspective from a doubtful one to a winning one, and bring out what you have to offer to others- which will bring you out to be a likeable person with any crowd, right off the bat. I want you to think of it as a visual reminder that promotes charisma and confidence. It's this simple;

Get a piece of paper and a pen, and set aside about ten to twenty minutes, free of distraction. Set the timer, make sure it doesn't exceed the twenty minutes, so that you don't start thinking too hard or crossing things. Start by writing down as many things as you can about your personality that you admire, that you're proud of and simply make you, 'you'. You could think of things like your love for taking pictures, or your past experiences with traveling the world. Don't forget to add experiences you've had that set you apart, this part could be personal or professional. Add to it lessons you've learnt so far, perspectives on different areas of your life, what you have learnt so far about people, love, the opposite sex and yourself. You can update the list over the next week or two. Tape it up on to your bedroom wall or wardrobe and look at it every day. Keep reminding yourself how great you are, and how awesome you've become, how smart and wise different life experiences has made you. Make sure to read your list at least twice a day. Trust me, this list won't just remind you that you're that kind of person who deserves to be well liked, soon it will become internalized in you, so that whatever limiting disturbances you may have about yourself, can virtually become eradicated- this is just to give you the ability to attract much more better experiences to yourself. I guess you didn't know this, but your body tends to respond based on your social interactions. We are social animals, we are born and hard wired to live in groups of between 100 and 200 people.

Our memories are basically formed based on the number of people that exist in an average person's social life. Haven't you thought about feeling more creative at a coffee shop surrounded by perfect strangers, even when you have headphones on? Or more powerful after going on a date with someone you particularly like? It all boils down to neurologically impact of social interaction- the discharge of dopamine that takes place when another human being gives you positive feedback, maybe a laugh at your joke, a slap on the back, or another request to spend more time together. Your body has been designed to literally feed on it, in turn making likeability to likely occur. You want to be liked and your instincts will do what it can to make that happen.

## Impacts of likeability

The only thing that should be on your mind, as you read this book, is to start thinking about how people see you along with the decisions and choices they make about you. By getting to know what those choices are and how they are made, you can set up a sixth sense about what does and does not work in presenting yourself to other people. The idea being that, when you fully get to understand the way your presence affects others, you'll be able to manipulate your actions to get the results you want. Even though you feel that sounds manipulative, it doesn't have to be all tweak. Just like any tool, it's all in how make use of it.

If you decide to go down the road of manipulation, yes, likability can be much more of a tool, but I would say a big part of likability is having that power and strength and bot making use of it. I could put a full book about the benefits of being likable, but I guess you already have a goal to meet in mind, because I believe you wouldn't be reading this right now if you didn't. So what I want to do now is open up a little secret for you- one of the most profound secrets that likable people everywhere hold over the mean, dormouse men and women that can't just get any attention. Likability isn't forced; it's organic- this means three things.

First, you have to feel the confidence inside of you that will make it happen. Ever watch a woman swing by in to a bar and have men flock to her in droves? Or a man who can seemingly get a date with just any lady? Yes, they are likeable, but beneath that, likeability seem to be something more- a feeling of self that transcends simple surface traits. They are certain about themselves and we are all moved and intoxicated by that powerful feeling of sense of self. That's you- you have to be 100% confident about the time if you want to be remotely successful in the likeability world. Here are some secrets I've used for years- and my notion has always been if it can work on someone like me and other likeable people I've come across, then it can work for you.

- **Get out of your comfort zone- just a little bit**

I can guess what you're thinking right now- you feel you'll be the most confident person in the world by now if being confident was really that easy. But the truth is, most of the time, we tend to make it harder on ourselves than it has to be. This has been able to be a part of you because you spend about 60% of your day with unfocused thoughts- thoughts that wander from "what time it is"to"how best I can make my presentation for that client more captivating", to "I wish I was eating pizza right now".

This truth is, you don't really have to consume all your energy on thoughts that don't make sense. You can actually 'do' something instead of 'think' about it, until you catapult in to a confident person within a very short time. The way to this is simply by stepping outside of your comfort zone, just a little bit. If you're used to doing the same thing during the weekend, and as a result you run into the same people over and over again, making you feel like there isn't anyone to date or talk to, or new people to get to know. Now is the time to create a profile that shows off your most confident, happy self; for instance, write about how you love try new stuffs, heading to music festivals or trying new restaurants, etc.

- **Smile, and give someone a compliment**

Think about it- when was the last time you got a compliment from someone? Chances, you probably might not remember. Most people don't come from a giving side of mind, because most people are so consumed by their own lives that they find it so difficult to step outside of themselves, and enjoy the person and/ or the moment for what it is. One thing you have to note is how you'll gain confidence and credibility as a person, around all what you may be going through, when you stop by, smile and give someone a compliment. It could come as simple like, "I love that gown, where did you get it?" or, it could be something like, "I feel much more better after you showed me that little secret about my excel spreadsheet, thanks!" complements make people feel better, especially when they know it's actually a sincere one, that's when they are not able to pick up on inauthentic statements. When you make people feel good, they'll surely associate you with feeling good. Imagine a secret skill that would make you become more popular than you could have ever hoped for.

- **Become a skilled daydreamer**

I would want you to emulate this also; it's always good when you make use of your mind to achieve what you want most in life- that sounds like the first step to likeability and success. Maybe you want to have an active dating life, a thriving career, the ability to become fit and thin, or establish a happier and more harmonious relationship with your partner, becoming a skilled daydreamer is your lifeline there. Here's why; your subconscious mind is filled with different thoughts, emotions and attitudes, many of which you might have learnt while observing others or getting to know more about life. Unfortunately, some of these feeling and thoughts, emotions and attitudes are negative and quite limiting. A thought may come as; "it doesn't look like I'll ever lose this weight, so why even try?" These subconscious feelings and thoughts guide our actions and in turn dictate our behaviors. It can stop us from making more money, better opportunities, and a greater love.

But here's the good news, you can actually fight and change your subconscious thoughts by re- programming your conscious mind. You can do this by becoming a self- proclaimed "daydreamer at the pro level" I bet your friends and colleagues will laugh at you, wait until you start getting financial opportunities they would only dream of. By focusing on just one image in your mind, maybe imagining yourself playing basketball with a whole team of people who happen to be your good friends, you can convince yourself that, in fact, you have this in your life and you can improve your confidence about it. The first step to doing this is by coming up with one basic ideal image- something you desire to have in your life- and imagine it over and over. Dream about it, with intentions as though it's actually happening in reality, several times a day. Do more of this if you can, trust me, it will really help. The second step to improving your confidence through daydreaming is simply visualizing it while believing it. In other words, you really do not have to go through the motions and lament, "aw, it sure would be nice to have an amazing in my life" have the belief that it's happening right now, as though you are the miracle worker in your own life with the magic wand. You have your dreams right in your hands, so you have  the power to either manifest them or block them form coming through in your life right now. Daydream by placing focus on the emotion. So if you wish to have the confidence to make a whole  lot of people laugh, dream about speaking to others, and listening to their laughter echo to the room. Watch their smiling faces, and imagine yourself to be the powerful, comedic presence in their life- and as an individual they can depend on to feel much better, based your confidence to stand and tell a great joke, or to be a skilled storyteller. Trust me, repetition really works, capture and picture the image of what you want in your mind, and learn to dream with intentions, having at the back of your kind that whatever it is that you want to accomplish, will definitely come true. It's just a daydream away. For you to become credible, it's important that stop worrying about what others think. More specifically, you have to let go of the thoughts that have been plaguing you since the last outing you made. Did someone make jest of you regarding your hobbies? Ignore you altogether? Forgot your name? Trust me, it doesn't matter. When you come across someone for the first time, they will make a series of snap judgments about the kind of person you are and whether they really want to strike a conversation with you. If you remain in that position to worry about the mistakes you've made, they'll keep on judging that same mistake prone person you were weeks or months ago- just let it go. Be someone interesting, exciting and above all- new. That's when you can build a rapport that will influence likability.

# CHAPTER 2

## LIKABILITY AND WHAT PEOPLE THINK ABOUT YOU

Do you even think about it? What people really think about you? I guess it's what you do almost every time you engage in a conversation with people, but now I'm going to disclose something that goes against every emotion you've felt since you were six years old- it doesn't matter, what people really think about you doesn't really matter, and here's why. When you come across someone for the first time, one of these three things happen often:

- They will show interest in what you have to say and will definitely want to listen to more of it.
- Your personality or mannerisms will put them off so they'll stop paying attention.
- You'll just stick to see what you're all about when you find out that they are too busy or simply unsure of you.

In short, I would just conclude that they'll have a strong positive, strong negative or neutral feeling or reaction toward you. I've heard and seen cases of people that are fearful of that strong negative reaction- so much that they'd avoid contact altogether. I know you might be going through that too as well; it's an actual phobia- that fear of instant rejection. Scientists around the world have resolved to calling it social phobia- this, if you let it grow may cripple your privileges and ability to meet new people, talk to the people you already know and generally place yourself out there to be part of the bigger discourse. In short, it's very bad. But, our focus in this book goes far beyond all that. Our aim is to set up a situation in which you get to know for a fact that you are being genial and likable, but more importantly, you will have the courage to stand on your feet and say "who cares" if someone shows that strong negative reaction to you. You have to understand that it's only people with low self- esteem that get worked when someone decides they don't like them. *This is who you are- the whole person that you are proud of and confident in. if you make the decision of changing that person and switching to someone different other than who you have always been, what then is the point of being a unique individual?* Believe me, but this is so true- when you're a whole, complete person with an interesting life and a magnetic personality, the last thing that would occur to you will be "what does this perfect stranger think about me?"

I know at this point you want to have a rethink, but why not practice the confident tips you have learnt, and be able to confidently assert who you are, without apologies. But, we are not yet there, and I understand your concern. These interactions and feelings might be more than just normal encounters at a grocery store. They could have a direct impact on your work and social status for months, and maybe even years to come. Now is the time to change your view about your social interactions for good, with magnetic personality.

- **Sexual confidence**

One thing for sure is innately attractive about a likeable person. For now, ignore everything you see on TV about the rude, mean people who seem to get all the men or women. Now, I'm talking about something out of the line, something different and unique- I'm about sexiness; sex appeal. With experiences from clients I've coached and numerous researches that have been carried out, we've able to deduct that sex appeal is all about confidence. You really do not have to be manipulative before you'll get what you want, you really do not have to be mean, there's really no need to puff out your feathers or put on designer clothes to get the attention of the opposite sex. Complaining to get more sex, affection or thoughtful gestures of appreciation shouldn't be your focus- or has any of that ever worked anyways? The secret about sex appeal is that no matter the sex you are- either you're a man or a woman, it comes to a sensual and a sexual confidence. This sense of confidence is so attractive and magnetizing because it tends to draw people in, and it does this because these people that possess it are in control of their reality. They sit down to analyze, to dictate what will happen to them at every step of a relationship. You're not wrong, we all want a partner that is intelligent and sure of their self, but everyone wants a partner who is nice to spend time with. They insist on getting someone with a good sense of humor, someone who can go on with a conversation, ask for an opinion, and generally engage anyone they come across. These kind of people are strong, sure of themselves, true and clear in their intentions. Even though they have boundaries, they are still open minded enough to carry on and enjoy life- no matter the circumstance that may arise. They control and take care of their physical and emotional needs, without waiting on anyone to do it for them.

And just because of this, they are able to radiate sex appeal to everyone they come across. I'm quite sure one out of many of your wishes is to have the real secret that guides everlasting attraction- that type that doesn't just come and go, but stays put in your life… throughout for life? Now I'm going to give you your secret blueprint to showing off your best, most attractive self to others, which in turn will effortlessly and reliably bring about more love, passion and desire than you'll know what to do with!

- **Work with your femininity if you're a female**

This is what you inherently have in possession as a female- femininity. Trust me, being a woman is a great and very attractive thing, because at your core, you are giving nurturing and loving. You are kind and gentle, and also a care taker for your family. Most attractive of all, is the gift you've been given to feel emotions on a deep level and nurture your relationships- this is one thing men don't have an easy, or natural time to carry out. A lot of women make the mistake of hiding these traits, you really do not have to feel weak or vulnerable while in relationships. You can instantly become likeable, you can turn out to be someone who effortlessly magnetizes herself to men just by embracing who you are, and what you inherently offer. How to go about it is simple- you can work on your femininity by smiling, by opening yourself up to men, by showing them who you are, what experiences you've been through and what you've seen, touched and felt in your life. This does not mean that you have to act manipulative or angry in order to get what you want. You really shouldn't be that type to nag the man in your life in order to get him to change his behavior. Just be rest assured that your giving, loving demeanor is what will create a true flow, and an abundant outcome for your relationship. Try to concentrate on the things that you already possess as a woman- your deep ability to feel your emotions, your ability to love even though you feel vulnerable, and your big, giving heart. All these will team up to facilitate the attraction and desire in your romantic relationships.

- **Work with your masculinity as a male**

Being a man means a lot- you have something big and awesome at your disposal, the type that will immediately allow you to have a magnetizing kind of sex appeal that women will be drawn to for a lifetime; your masculinity. You have these things deposited in you- as a man you are naturally a protector, a provider and a skilled and a quick decision maker. You can make a quick decision on how to please your client, or to take care of your family. You are powerful and strong in your convictions, and you're honest and sharp in your communication. You're independently minded, intelligent and decisive. When you make use of this to your utmost ability, you become looked at as a strong, capable, and confident partner ladies are instantly drawn to. You're a knight in shining amour. So when you bring your natural traits to limelight in your relationship or dating life, and make yourself as someone who knows what he wants- this is auto magnetism at work. It's that simple- harnessing who you are at your core, in order to make the person in your life feel really good.

- **Accept the other person**

One other thing we've been able to come up with- most of the time, we doubt ourselves, or try too hard to get the person we want, or wonder how we'll keep the connection going. The truth is, it simply takes bringing our natural empowerments and strengths to limelight, while bringing theirs in at the same time. We've heard about those women who make the mistake of nagging, complaining or stonewalling (giving them the silent treatment and the likes) the man in their life as a punishment for him not giving her what she really deserved. Some men just 'tune' women out of the line with work, or sports watching on TV, instead of spending time in the relationship, just to make it better. The truth simply is, the more time you invest in your relationship, the better it becomes. The more consistent, thoughtful and mindful you are in regards to the other party, the more giving, mindful and thoughtful they will be with you. Let the person you're interested in that you are mentally, emotionally and physically invested. Just let them know that they'll all you're thinking about. Make it a part of you by sending messages like "I miss you, I'm thinking about you and I can't wait to see you"- trust me, these soft messages really work. When it comes to relationships- and cultivating an intensely passionate, and seriously satisfying relationship, and it requires is some care, attention and the nurturing of the small details stated.

Get ready; this isn't just about being likable- it's about showing off the perfect version of yourself in a way that will become irresistible to everyone you meet.

# CHAPTER 3

## BEING LIKEABLE BY NOT BEING UNLIKABLE- HOW DOES THAT SOUND?

Sit back and think for a moment- about the last time you came across someone you didn't like. What can you remember about them? Was it how silent they were or how they didn't flow in the conversation? I doubt it. More than likely, the last person you can think of not liking was boorish, obnoxious and rude. There are two kinds of people who are not liked by others- those that do not make an impressions and therefor are not proactively liked or disliked and those who seem to be so obnoxious or rude that they instantly push you away from them. And to put things in view, you really do not have to be that obnoxious to be unlikable- in reasonable and polite company, it doesn't take much. The truth about it is- you cannot be likable if you do not learn how not to be unlikable. Everything that has been put together in this book focuses on helping you stand out, be confident and interesting. But, none of all that has been said does any good if you happen to take jabs at people you do not really know, make degrading comments, or generally assume the worst about someone you just met. Most of the time, these things are merely bad habits. Other times, we find out that they are the result of lot of cynicism built up over years of poor skills. Whatever the problem may be, socialism starts with friendliness, and that's a bit harder for some of us than for others.

### The power of friendship

Less than 8 years ago, researchers studied about 24 students at the University of Virginia, taking them to the base of a steep hill and fitting them with a weighed backpack. The task was to estimate the steepness of the hill. Some of the participants stood beside their friends during the exercise, while others stood alone. At the end of the exercise, the students who stood with friends gave lower estimates of the steepness of the hill, and the longevity of the friendship also determine how the estimate appeared (the less steep the hill the appeared for friends from way back).

Maybe it's time for you to try a little harder so you can be a little better. The basic key to understand on the road to likability is recognizing the traits that stand out as being unlikable. Think of that thing you're doing now that could make someone else cringe or stop listening, I can say, for personal experience, that you probably don't realize you're doing any of them. Eliminate such thinking that just because you're some kind of social savant with the people who do like you that you don't have any bad habits. You only can know when you ask your friends or family. I'm sure they'll be able to point out the things on this list that go with your personality and probably offer you more than a dozen tips on how to fix the problem. There are a lot of things you never want to do to someone you adore and respect, especially if your aim is for them to like you. We've been able to come up with a list of *rude and unfriendly workplace behaviors*, they are things you should stop doing immediately:

- **Taking credit for someone else's work**

When your partner does something or broaches a topic, why not give them credit for the idea. One of the simplest ways we end a conversation in this case is saying "oh, yes, I heard that the other day and I also heard…." Then moving on as if you brought up the topic. This happens to be a bad habit many people have as they try to be engaging in conversation but it generally stops or alienates other people from speaking.

- **Discrimination or stereotyping**

It's this simple; don't say anything rude about someone else's race, gender, age, sexual orientation, or any other differences. It's actually rude, closed minded and will almost always offend someone nearby. Discrimination goes a bit even further- if your decision is based only on the key elements, you may be discriminating. This is one big thing to look out for in dating.

- **Talking down to other people**

This one appears to something common among us- talking down to someone in a position you assume "lower" than yourself is a sure way to alienate every new person you come across. Just because you have some people bagging your groceries does not mean they are less intelligent or interesting than you. They could be your good friend or spouse, but talking down will create an uncomfortable situation every time you set eyes on each other.

- **Inappropriate jokes or mocking**

Mocking people or making unnecessary jokes is unfriendly in any situation. The only exception should be if you already know someone, that's when you can establish that kind of relationship and be sure that they will not be offended. Even at that, be sure to gauge the limits of your jokes, because it's very easy to go too far and create an uncomfortable scenario.

- **Littering and General messiness**

Just as your hairdo and clothing make statements about your self- esteem and confidence level, your overall cleanliness in your car, office or home will explain a lot about the kind of person that you are. Next time you're out with someone, look around for a garbage can for your empty coffee cup, not the bottom of a ditch.

- **Use of technology while engaging in a conversation**

Nothing is less friendly than taking out a cell phone or checking your watch while having a conversation. These interactions have unspoken subtext like "this is far more important than our conversation". It will definitely upset anyone you are spending time with and will make you seem like you don't really care about their input.

- **Patronizing**

There is one common thing about some parents, especially the impatient ones. Just because a six year old boy needs a bit of help understanding a new concept does not mean your co- workers or a person you stumbled on in the bar need to be talked to like that. It's somewhat unintentional nine out of ten times, but also the effect is just as unfriendly.

- **Eye Rolling and Sarcasm**

Think about it; if someone you just met rolled their eyes at a statement you uttered or started making sarcastic statement about you or your conversation. How long would you hang around and continue talking to them? Most of the time, people try to be playful or charming with sarcasm. It sometimes doesn't work, so stay with easy things like non- personal jokes.

- **Whining and Complaining**

This acts may not seem unfriendly, but doing them even if it's unrelated to the person you're having a conversation to will give the wrong impression. Whining and complaints make a lot of people either uncomfortable or upset. On the flip side, if you can maintain a positive tone while having a conversation, people will feed on your positivity and will also want to be around you more often.

- **Unnecessary angry outbursts or yelling**

To a lot of people, general anger is a turnoff. It simply shows a lack of self-control, a short fuse, and a tendency to judge other people and events without all the facts. If you have a habit of getting angry at random events, take a step back and relax before starting a conversation. Stay with positive actions and activities. Friendliness isn't difficult. It's probably the easiest thing you'll learn as you flow along.

So, stepping out and talking to strangers can be a very difficult task at the beginning, but nothing to worry yourself about, I've put up some really ice-breakers, and exercises to help you carry on with that:

- **Kill them with kindness, every time**

Your aim is to be more neighborly with your neighbor? Or you want to be able achieve a greater comradery at work- genuine kindness should be your main key that I've found to work out well, that's one thing that gets people to come together with a common goal. Giving a compliment is one way to bring others together. Offering to solve an issue is another important way to close up the gap between you and others.

- **Engage in small talk like a pro**

If you find yourself at a work related dinner party, or a social one, you can just easily start up a small talk with others around you. At first, you might feel nervous, but that's okay. You might make the huge menu what you're overwhelmed about, something like; "have you ever seen so many salad options before? I haven't" would be good, or you can talk about anything related to the meal you're taking at the moment, or the restaurant you're dining at. What about something like- "I've never had Cuban food before, what about you? It has always been my dream to go there, have you travelled much?" stepping out of your comfort zone to play a sport or join a club or meet someone in a bar- those might be hard. Being friends with someone you just met? That's as easy as it gets. It just takes a different world perspective.

**Something's got you riled up?**

Nine times of ten, the rudeness we show to others is not seen. No, you shouldn't just be a pushover, but is there really a need to yell at the man/woman in Starbucks after a 5 minute wait in line? It's not their fault and they certainly cannot do anything about it. You could just as easily have made friends by telling a joke or making them feel better about what is most likely a stressful day, but instead you got rode and only made things worse. Anger is one of those agents that can severely interrupt even a good conversation. Have you ever had a partner or someone you're dating get angry while driving in the car? It's so uncomfortable. How is it always like? They yell, bang on the steering wheel, swear and do all sort of things that you'd never do in front of someone from whom you want to gain respect. Even at that when you love that person, it's uncomfortable and slightly embarrassing. Now imagine doing that to a stranger, and think of how they'd react to it as well.

**Reducing unfriendliness**

*"The only way that you can live, is if you grow, the only way that you can grow is if you change, the only way that you can change is if you learn, the only way that you can learn is if you are exposed. And the only way that you can become exposed is if you throw yourself out in to the open. Just do it, throw yourself"*. Let's assume that you are a relatively nice person, you don't get overly angry at anything in particular, and you can always start and keep up with a decent conversation for at least a few minutes. So, why then? Why do you still come off as unfriendly? No, you're not broken, this isn't a personality disorder and you definitely don't need pills. To be more realistic, you're not even trying to be unfriendly- I'd call it a combo of insecurity and discomfort in the presence of others that is causing your unfriendliness and nine times out of ten, simply getting to know that discomfort will help to reduce it. Over the years, I've been able to come up with three "don't do" communication pitfalls, I'm sure it would work for you too as it would allow you to mend the 'disconnect' in your relationship, repair any miscommunication that has recently taken place, and also communicate

feelings of respect, admiration and appreciation for my partner. No matter what type of relationship you're in to- a romantic one, a professional one or a personal one (maybe with a family member, a neighbor, a parent at your kid's preschool, etc.) getting rid of these following pitball can drastically heighten your popularity, improve your ability to get along with everyone and reduce social blunders that can affect your social life.

## Being defensive

One of the fastest steps you can take to emotionally distance your partner from you is by putting him or her on the defense. Saying things to your partner like "why would I want to make you feel this way? I didn't do it on purpose!" or "why haven't you asked me how I'm feeling when you know I've had a bad day today?" makes your partner feel like they are under attack. Being in a relationship is simply about being on the same team, and sticking together. When times are rocky. It far from picking fights and playing on opposite teams or positioning yourself against the other. Anytime you blame your partner for something, they feel backed in to a corner, and as if nothing they utter has an effect against what you're saying. So, instead of you using "you" messages such as "do you always have to take your friend's side against mine? Or "you never tell me how good I look anymore" why not make use of the "I" messages. These messages are incredibly powerful and strong, because they remove any opportunity for your partner to feel blamed, and instead create a statement of how you're feeling- which is hard for anyone to deny or fight against, as it's simply the way you feel.

## Insulting your partner

Are you in a relationship in which you always fight dirty? If so, using a language full of insults is one of the easiest ways to turn your relationship in to a destructive one and possibly headed for a breakup. A lot of other people prefer to call it contempt, insulting your partner is any tune or behavior that seem threatening, demeaning or below the belt- maybe comments that push their buttons. Embarrassing or insulting the other party puts you at war against him/her instead of working together to bring out a solution. The problem is, when you make use of contempt against your partner in a relationship, all rules are out of the window. The name calling can start. The physical or emotional threats can bring up a whole new standard for fighting- now and for the future of your relationship. The pattern and sense of respect, confidence, admiration and appreciation your partner felt is now gone.

Perhaps worse of all, it tends to set a new standard for your relationship- that at any time, you can declare war, and for any reason on your partner- because contempt is an emotional, irrational state to be in. contempt can be somewhat degrading, such as comments like "you're a fool. Why would you think I would want you to engage in that?" or eyes rolling after your partner says a grammatically incorrect sentence. The undertone of that appears to be a clear message of "you're stupid, and I'm smart", or 'you're correct and I'm wrong."

That simple, you change how you talk, communicate and address your feelings in a relationship before they pose a negative impact. Even when you're not in good agreement, you can still contribute something positive and help mend the 'disconnect' without calling names, threats or negative body language. One important thing to be aware of is your micro- body expression that explains what you're really thinking to your partner, before you even say it out. It could be learning to monitor the way you roll your eyes, or a frown you make every time you notice your partner doing something you don't approve of. Or, you could try this other way out- take a deep breath before you speak, so that you calm to sensor what you want to say so you can assess it before actually spilling it out.

**Stonewalling**

Probably you might not have heard of the term, stonewalling, before, but I bet there's a good chance you've participated in it a time or two. It's simply when one person is upset, communicating or trying to explain their viewpoint on something, and you get off them by ignoring them, or "shutting them out". If you're doing the stonewalling, it could be because you're so frustrated, that the only behavior you think might get the attention you want is by ignoring that they are even in the area at that time. But, for the individual that is being stonewalled, it feels like they are being ignored, and that their position in the relationship is being invalidated. Have you ever given someone the silent treatment before? Yes- most times, we are all guilty of it a time or time. Unfortunately, stonewalling someone does not solve anything, and of course it can cause the other person to become more defensive. One thing you can do is to practice active listening- I mean the one you wouldn't have to react emotionally. Give the person the chance to say whatever it is they want to say, just show that you're listening by nodding or saying, "I understand" and then responding by repeating back what they think they just said. You can study breaking the stonewalling pattern altogether by helping the person who is doing the stonewalling to come to a less emotional state. Ask those questions, using positive statements to calm down by saying things like, "I know you're angry and I want to help us come around a solution as quickly as I can, so that we can both be happy again."

# CHAPTER 4

## MAKING OUT FOR THE CONFIDENCE MACHINE

*"Maybe it's high time we tried the impossible"* hop on any book that's all about getting along with people- any single book, whether it's on dating, getting ahead at work, or just making new friends- and you'll notice one common trait on top of the list. The single most important trait is always confidence and it will always will be. On the other note, when you do not have so much confidence in your social abilities, you'll start to think things like "what if I say the wrong thing" or "what does she think about me?" so, to fully detach your interactions with people and conversations from the constant connection to yourself, you have to be confident. You should look good, feel good and be sure that everything you say is 100% what you think and believe- with no regrets. Even if someone doesn't like what you say or do, you have to feel confident enough to move on quickly, learning from all sorts of mistakes you make and pushing to the next interaction. That's hard, actually. It's extremely hard and it's also one of the reasons why people skip this final step completely. They only go about, reading books about how to dress, stand and talk and yet forget how important it is to overhaul how they think about pretty much everything. This is exactly where I am going to start and it should be an important part of your magnetic personality plan form the ground plan.

**Improving yourself.**

I really don't care about what your goal is; if you look messy and therefore feel unattractive, you're definitely going to have hard time boosting your confidence. This isn't about being "unattractive"- I don't mean that in the manner that other people don't innately find you appealing. I mean dirty, unkempt, or generally messy- the things that you can turn around with relative ease and just haven't. Trust me, the last thing on my mind right now is to put a dent in your self- esteem when trying to improve it, but we have to start somewhere, so right now, I need to you to be 100% honest and sincere with yourself. Do you really feel and look good as you want to? Or are there certain things you'd like to improve and polish up a bit? This seems to be a tricky subjective area, because I honestly feel that no one actually needs to change who they are to meet others. However, I do have the feeling that the human body has been designed as an advertisement for how we feel about ourselves. When you see a person putting on ratty sneakers with dirt under their nails, faded clothes, and unkempt hair, what comes to your mind first? What do you think about such person first? It's probably that such individual in front of you doesn't think very highly of themselves and their body accordingly. This only does not affect how people see you, it also affects how you see yourself. When you put on your finest clothes, fix your hair, take a shower, and step out, I guess you'll probably feel a lot better about yourself, at least at a subconscious level. This is a natural reaction. So a big part of boosting your morale is developing good habits and activities that will help you honestly feel much better about yourself.

**Taking good care of your body and mind**

The first thing is to take good care of yourself. This may not pinch every reader, but I'll wager a guess that most of you reading this right now have at least a partial tendency to become lazy in this aspect of your life. And if your aim is to improve the way you'll be liked so you can easily meet someone of the opposite sex, or everyone entirely, then this part is even more important. I like it to be kept simple, so I recommend you do the same. Why spend hundreds of dollars when you could spruce things up a bit and back up the package up with an interesting person on the inside. That's our goal remember. I'm not trying to whitewash the real you. I just want to light it up for presentation.

- **Hair**

Hair simply needs to be taken good care of. You don't need a $200 hair cut or a fancy wave in to impress the people around you. But, ratty, overly long, untrimmed hair isn't going to work. Keep your hair kept well and trim any unsightly bodily hair is often as possible.

- **Clothing**

Put on appropriate clothing for the situation. Going to a party for work? Put on something spiffy and professional. You want to go to a beach to relax your muscles? Why not get a new swimsuit. Your style is just up to you, but be sure that your clothing is clean, appropriate and refreshing to look at.

- **Scent**

You really don't have to pour on the perfumes or cologne unless you know what you are doing, but at least start up with some deodorant and a nice body wash to cover up any unsightly odors that may come up while dancing or going about your work on a sunny day.

- **Feet**

If its shoes you want to put on, polish those puppies up and keep them in good shape. When you notice that the shoes start tearing, ripping or falling apart, make sure to replace them. Your focus should be on your external appearance every day, working to create a finely tuned, confident shell for the interesting, likable you on the inside.

- **Fitness**

Weight is not all that important. It really isn't. But fitness can definitely make a difference. This simply means the ability to walk a few miles without feeling exhausted in any way. You should be able to keep up with every one you meet. Fitness does not only make you feel better about yourself, it will also help you physically and emotionally when you want to go in to conversations with positive mindset.

# CHAPTER 5

## LEARNING NEW SKILLS

You might have heard about Dale Carnegie favorite quote where he said it isn't who you are or where you are or what you are doing that makes you happy or unhappy, it's simply what you think about it. This is so true because it's one secret to winning friends and influencing people positively. There are skills you can use, about a library of cool things you can do that other people would wish they could do. Without a good base of skills, you'll start comparing yourself to other people in ways that isn't healthy. Trust me, it's a bad habit to start with, but in a situation where you do not have anything to show off and feel confident about, it can be very difficult to see through that constant, nagging feeling that you're not as perfect as the people that you go around with. The solution is just simple- why not learn new skills? Get out there and learn how to make things happen, how to do things that will make you more interesting and confident in your doing. Don't get confused at this point, I'm generalizing for a good reason. You can literally learn how to make anything happen and draw interest from the people you meet, the point to consider here is diversity, not outrageousness.

**What are you good at already?**

Ask yourself the question; what are you good at? There should be something that you do better than people that you're familiar with, or those that you have always been very good at. Discover the special ability and activity and find ways to increase it.

If you're good at running, why not get out there and play a sport with a lot of running like Soccer or Basketball – you'll have something more interesting to talk about with anyone who plays those sports and other athletes you love in general. If you love to sing, head straight over to your local bar on karaoke night and sing your heart out, everything gets better!  If you love to paint, write or draw, leave out one day of the week to devote to what you know how to do best. The more you focus on special attributes and gifts you love, the more love you can bring into your life, simply because you're auto-magnetizing people to you. The truth is, people are drawn to others who are energized, passionate and happy. The more you focus on what you love to do, the greater you'll be able to attract other people to you.

**Learn How to Describe Your Skills**

When you meet someone for the first time, it's easy to be glad about what you can now offer, but introducing it should be carried out in a way that draws them into conversation – not through bragging. A lot of people love to share what they think and help you succeed in your endeavors. Don't cut them off when they try to add to the talk, just because you develop a skillset doesn't mean you're a guru who can walk around telling people what to believe or think about it.   There are a lot of skills and personal development opportunities out there. Just to give you a glimpse of how likeable of a person you can become, here are a few of my favorites:

- **Learn a new and different Language** – Learning a new language is one of the most effective ways to meet new people and become likeable instantly. Not only does it allow you open yourself up to an entire world of individuals who don't speak your native tongue, you will also have the chance to meet other people trying to learn whatever language you have interest in, it is a nice addition to what you already know.
- **Play a Sport** – Physical activity is for more than just skill development. It helps you to stay active, helps you feel good about yourself, and gives you the chance to show off how skilled you can be with a synthetic ball or how funny you can be when you fall. Sports are one of the greatest ways to meet and get along new people, even if you're on the look-out for a date, these skills you're about to develop can be applied to pretty much anything else you enjoy.
- **Read About a Topic** – Reading does not seem like a good way to meet people directly, but it does something exceptional- helping you build up a nice knowledge base that can be tapped in any conversation. If you've ever been trapped in a dull, dragging conversation with a stranger who doesn't even know the

difference between the President of France and George Clooney, you know that having at least a basic pool of understanding will make you infinitely more interesting to such people you've just met.

- **What about writing a Book or Poetry** – Writing is another fantastic way to develop your skills. While I don't usually advise going around showing off your writing knowledge, simply being agile with your pen alone makes you more effective in communicating ideas to other people, be it in email, in conversation or over the phone.

- **Go camping or Hiking** – Roughing it in the great outdoors opens up a number of doors to other people willing to go through them, and now they'll be left with no choice than to do it with you. Hiking and camping aren't for everyone thought, but venturing outdoors can add up with a lot of fun things to do on the weekend. Not only that, getting to meet fellow outdoorsy people is incredibly easy, once you get into the swing of the trend.

- **Learn How to Paint** – If you'd like to develop yourself on more aesthetic skills, painting or crafting in the comfort of your home can be a great way to develop a connection with the texture and feel of your world, thus, bringing in people of interest to like your work and you. Even non-artistic types are free to go down this path with model car kits or electronics kits.

- **Learn to Play a special Instrument** – An instrument is simply an instant conversation starter. And while some instruments are harder than others to learn, you can pick up a guitar for less than $200 at the shop and learn how to pick out some basic tunes with an hour or two, you'd definitely get better with constant practice.

- **Learn to Cook** – Cooking is fun, popular, and incredibly healthy for you if prepared the right way. Being able to talk about food, offer recipes, and talk about your recent concoctions can generate a huge opening in meeting new people that'll develop interest in you.

- **Study Plants and Gardening** – Gardening is relaxing and offers plenty of opportunities to learn more about the outside world. People will talk about gardening with you; trust me on that.

- **Fix up Your Home** – Home repair and improvement is another great way to get out and use your hands. It also offers you the chance to once again attract attention in your neighborhood and build up a great reputation.

If you're looking out to making new friends with something interesting to say, take a stab at any one of the things on this list, or better yet, step out there and look for an interest that goes with your personality. Believe me, anything works for this – it only takes the right dedication to make it happen.

**Self-Image and Self-Talk**

How do you go about those obnoxious voices? How do you shut them up for good, or better yet, replace them with positive voices that can encourage you through even the toughest social encounters?

It's simple- **Through positive imaging and self-talk.**

For as long as I've been an adult, I've studied MIND POWER EXERCISES that sting into the innate ability we all have to talk ourselves into an optimistic outlook on life. And the best part is that it's actually as simple as it sounds. Here's the idea.  Our brains are very powerful, very intricate machines, but they have been designed to handle so much "reality". So, if the world around us is significantly different than how we see it, our brains will try to close the gap and make things match up to how they seem, to suit you. This is called cognitive dissonance, and self-starters have been making use of it for centuries to create a positive mind set and make seemingly impossible goals come true.

**Working on self esteem**

Did you know? Confidence is built on a firm foundation of self-esteem. You have to feel good about yourself before you can honestly say to yourself "everything is possible" and better yet, show that confidence to a perfect stranger.  But, self-esteem is as notoriously tough trait to bring back when life has battered you around of late.  It's one of those things that come as much out of your environment as from within. It's incredibly difficult to feel good about yourself if you're feel bad about yourself. So, to fight that kind of thinking, you'll need to make a few changes in you.

# CHAPTER 6

## CREATING A POSITIVE MIND SET

Positivity! That's the simple word and also one of the most powerful things you'll learn in this book. You can't just wake up one day and go buy positivity like you would a new pair of shoes. You can't have your negative mentality cut off like a mop of shaggy hair. You have to build it up from within, generating sincere, positive power deep inside that your subconscious mind can thrive on. When you wake up each day, don't forget to remind yourself of the positive influences in your world and the opportunities that await you, things open up – you'll feel a surge of energy unlike anything you've come across before. Check out a few things to know, and be sure that you're just a step ahead to becoming the most likeable person in your world;

- **Make use of positive words alone when talking** – Focus on saying things in positive ways, even when you're describing a negative situation. It will help you think and focus of solutions and better yet understand what other people's actions are caused by- this is very important.
- **Repeat your affirmations daily** – Get those affirmations straight and meditate on them day after day. Once you feel an affirmation has taken hold, get hold of new ones and continue to improve yourself on them.
- **Concentrate thoughts to positive imagery** – Images and visualization have great impact on how we think. Move your mind set from negative words to positive images, even if those images are not related to what you're trying to do at that moment.
- **Forgive yourself for mistakes from the past** – Your past is a fickle mistress who will come back to haunt you time and again. Instead of disturbing yourself about the effects of what has come before, why not forgive yourself and learn to live your life in the present?
- **Visualize negative thoughts turning into positive** – Here's a strategy that works wonders for negative thoughts. When you have a negative thought, visualize it in your head and then slowly relate it into a positive image instead. Create an ideal image and work

toward it, this is a common neuro-linguistic programming exercise. In it, you get to visualize your ideal self – the perfect version of you that you want to present to other people around you. Then, you visualize yourself as you currently see yourself and carefully work toward shifting your mental image of one or two scenarios at a time to the ideal self. For example, if you're concerned about your weight, you should visualize your ideal weight and your current weight and then slowly change how you think of yourself to be closer to that ideal image you've envisioned- just simple.

- **List reasons you will be successful** – Make a list of ways and reasons you will find success in your life. Be as specific and realistic as possible.
- **Surround yourself with positivity** –Surround yourself with positive energies only, this, I'm sure you can easily do. Images on your computer, tapes with affirmations on them, and books with positive messages will help you stay positive at all time.
- **Track your thoughts and review them later** – Write down your thoughts as they come to you every day in a small notepad and then come back to them later to review what you were thinking and better yet, why you were thinking those things. This works because you can identify negative thoughts at a later date and determine if they were necessary to think about in the first instance.
- **Get rid of self-criticism** – Stop digging at yourself internally, you might not go far. Consider whether you've made the right decision or not and then move on. Think of ways to act better in the future, not to beat on yourself in the past.
- **Remove negative influences** – We already talked about this earlier, but you have to know that if someone is saying negative things to you or if you're surrounded by negative reinforcement, the best you can do is to get away from it.
- **Share with friends or a professional** – Be on the look- out for someone you can share both your negative and positive thoughts with. This can be your close friend, a spouse, or even a therapist that you would talk to on a regular basis.
- **Be nice to others** – This one is very simple and easy to comply to.

Be nice to other people and you'll feel more positive about yourself, even to those you didn't know before that time. Displaying negativity can create negative thoughts and make you to continue displaying negativity, this will hinder you from going forward.

- **Get inspiring input in books, movies, or poetry** – Find quotes, movies, music or other mediums that gives you inspiration. Keep them close by and review them when you need something to hold on to.

This is just a starter list – what will help you start thinking of the world in terms of what will help you find success.  But, it takes dedication. Positivity is harder for some people than others. A lot of us have been living in an 'if-then' world for too long. We think, "If this happens, then I'm just going to be dealing with that."  Why not start thinking in terms of "when-will". For you, the balance of your life should only be based on "when something happens, I will make something better happen". It's a powerful, affirmative attitude and it will help you to focus and remain positive even in the face of the worst possible situations.

### Reduce negative influences

While you're creating a positive mind set, it's equally important to cut all negativity attached to you. Some of it is internal, and you'll find that the more positive you become, the less negative thoughts will plague your days, but all those unsavory influences outside of you can place a serious dent in your new perspective if you're not observant and careful. This means you have to take a scalpel to the relationships that make you feel worst.  If you have a friend that constantly tells you how you cannot do something, or are in a romantic relationship with someone who is not in support of any of your hobbies or dreams, you either need to sit them down and have a chat about it or you need to completely remove them from your life.  There a lot of situations where negativity can opt in and ruin the way you view the world. But, that doesn't mean you cannot find success in those situations.  You have to learn to either get rid of those influences or give them less attention. When it is family or a loved one, you should pass across your desire to hear positive support, and if you cannot, limit the contact you have to ensure you are more success.

### Be on the look-out for like- minded people

Once you've been able to successfully cut out negativity in your life, then the next line of action is to replace it with people who get you. Lucky for you there is a whole book in stock to help you get through with that.  This comes in hand with time, but I want you to carefully consider every time you meet someone for the first time and denote what that person brings to your life. Do not selfishly think about what they can do for you – that's an act no one should dabble in to. Instead, think about how their behavior will affect your self-esteem and general approach to the outside world.  If they're constantly positive and honestly enjoying your company, then you've just got yourself a good friend. If they complain a lot and make you look down on yourself, then it's left for you to think about whether you really need to be friends with someone who makes you feel crummy.

## Stress Reduction

Right up there with negativity, stress is capable of putting a huge drain on your likability. Imagine what someone would think if they met you right after you finished working a 6 hour day, running errands and sitting in traffic for another hour. Would they be very interested in your new kickboxing hobby or would they just conclude that you're stressed? The last thing you wish is for stress to become a leading trait that defines the impression you make on others. It sure would make you cranky and generally unfriendly.  So, before stress gets a stranglehold on your social life, we're going to perform a little surgery on your cortisol output and calm your bones down with some simple, age old exercises.

## Meditation

*"The soul always knows how to heal itself. The challenge is to silence the mind." – Caroline Myss*

First up, there is the idea of physical extrication from stress.

If you exercise daily as I discussed a few page ago, then you're on a good path already. But, beyond simple fitness, you should take advantage of simple breathing exercises and meditation – one of civilization's oldest and most effective stress reduction principle.  There are many types of meditation, but I have always found relaxation and comfort in the simplest of breathing exercises.  The idea is very simple and easy. You relax, release the worries of the day and give yourself enough time to focus on the one important thing that matters most – "you".

- **Set aside a time every day** – Meditation is most effective when it becomes a standard part of your day. When your mind is rest assured for a fact that you'll be given the same 45+ minutes every day to relax and detach from all the stressful influences you've managed to carry over, it will fall into a much greater state of relaxation.
- **Sit in a comfortable position** – How you wish to meditate is up to you, but personally I always prefer to sit in a full lotus, with both feet curled beneath my legs into a cross legged position. You can also use a half lotus, which is placing one foot against the inside of your opposite thigh. Sitting is best because it allows you to focus only on the breathing exercise, not the act of walking. Lying down works for some people as well, but I tend to get sleepy, so I stay upright.
- **Breathe deeply** – Once you have been able to relax into a comfortable sitting position, breathe deeply through your nose. Pull the air slowly into your lungs, following the flow of the air into your nose, through your throat and into your lungs. Your diaphragm and stomach should go up with each breath, filling you up like a balloon. Hold the breath for a second and then release it, slowly letting the air gush out of your nose or mouth. The longer you breathe, the longer you should hold that breath. A relaxed body tends to make use of less oxygen and can relax into a perfect state. Daily meditation can help reduce stress, improve cognition, and provide you with a more intense knowledge and understanding of the world around you. Sleep where less air is needed. Concentrate on repeating this process over and over again, following those breaths into your body time and again.

This exercise, as simple as it sounds, is the very method used for centuries by some of the most enlightened bodies that ever lived to detach from the constant influx of worries and stressors in life. If you feel yourself losing the constant battle against stress, meditation can help equalize your strengths and overcome that feeling that you're losing it.

## Goal Keeping and Strength Development

Another easy way to cut down on stress is to outline and visualize all of your goals and strengths on a paper (or e-paper as the case may be). One of the leading causes of stress is scheduling. You have too much on your plate and you don't feel like there is enough time in the day to complete it all. So, instead of pushing yourself to the limit and then feeling inadequate for not getting it done, step back and think "what can I really get done today?

- **Goal tracking** – Number one on the list; keep track of the goals you have from day to day. Be realistic about how much you can get done from one moment to the next, and use goal setting software to create an outline of your day's necessities. Every goal you set should have actionable tasks you can complete, and specific tools you can use to generate successful results.
- **Develop strengths** – Everyone is good at some things more than others. Humans are unique in every way from each other and therefore are able to do things that others cannot. If you're not an athlete, you learned in school early that you should focus your energies on something more suited to your talents – academics, creativity, or something more immediately practical like shop. The same is true in your adulthood. Relax and find a way to recognize and then replicate your strengths in every part of your life.
- **Automate and relax** – Put it on autopilot and watch as your world becomes infinitely easier to manipulate and remain relaxed at the same time. Outsource tasks you don't have time to complete, delegate tasks at work, seek for help at home – whatever you need to do, ask yourself if there is a faster, more efficient way to do it. If there is, you'll save a tremendous amount of time and make your life infinitely easier and better.

Stress is a natural part of our life. It always will be.

When your child breaks their arm or you lose hours at work, you will be stressed out about it. It's only natural. But, when you're able to sit back and relax – understanding the purpose of that stress and why it is unnecessary, life becomes a lot easier, and you become a much more likable person to be around. It's just as simple as that, it's one thing for you to read and understand, it's another step to visualizing and making it all around, one way to be sure that you're on the right path is to follow everything that this book says- because in it, you have all it takes to become instantly likeable, you really do not need a therapist or a counsellor, you're just one step to being the best you've always dreamt of. Go on now and make it happen! It's in you! You have the potentials and the capability, nothing stops you! Nothing holds you back!